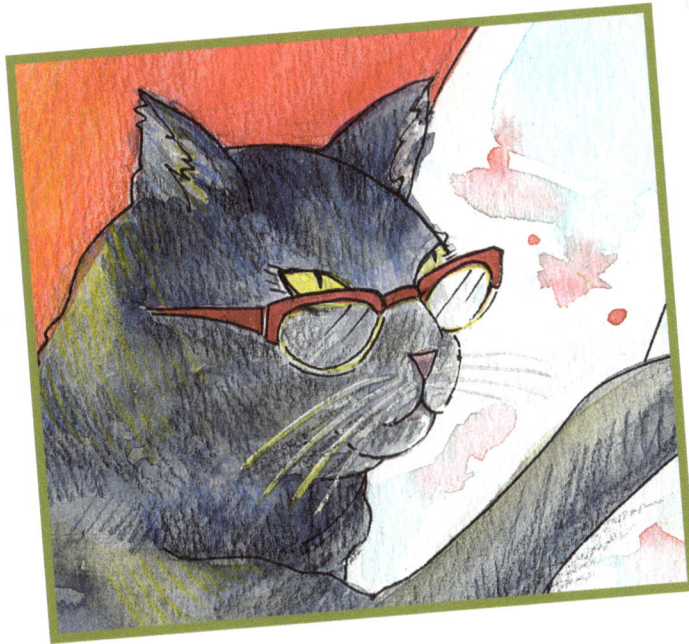

Mrs. Muggles
learns to read

Story by Penny Ross
Illustrations by Cathy Wickett

Butterfly Dreams Publishing

Library and Archives Canada Cataloguing in Publication

Ross, Penny, 1962-
Mrs. Muggles learns to read / Penny Ross; illustrator, Cathy Wickett.

Also issued in electronic format.
ISBN 978-0-9869033-5-9

I. Wickett, Cathy II. Title.

PS8635.0696M78 2012   jC813'.6   C2012-905250-7

Cover artwork and illustrations by Cathy Wickett, www.wickettdesign.com

Published by Butterfly Dreams Publishing
Box 1727, Gimli, Manitoba, Canada, www.butterflydreamspublishing.com

Printed and bound in the United States

For my nephews Tyler and Justin
May laughter and adventure guide your dreams

Special thanks to Grace Marteinsson, early years teacher
and Tanya Johannson, librarian for their guidance and suggestions.

**A glossary of words and a quiz can be found
on the last page of the story.**

Mrs. Muggles loves to read.

She likes to sit on a big red chair in a
sunny corner of the living room.

She can read there for hours.

Mrs. Muggles likes picture books.

They have big pages. It's easy to turn big pages.

Who is Mrs. Muggles?

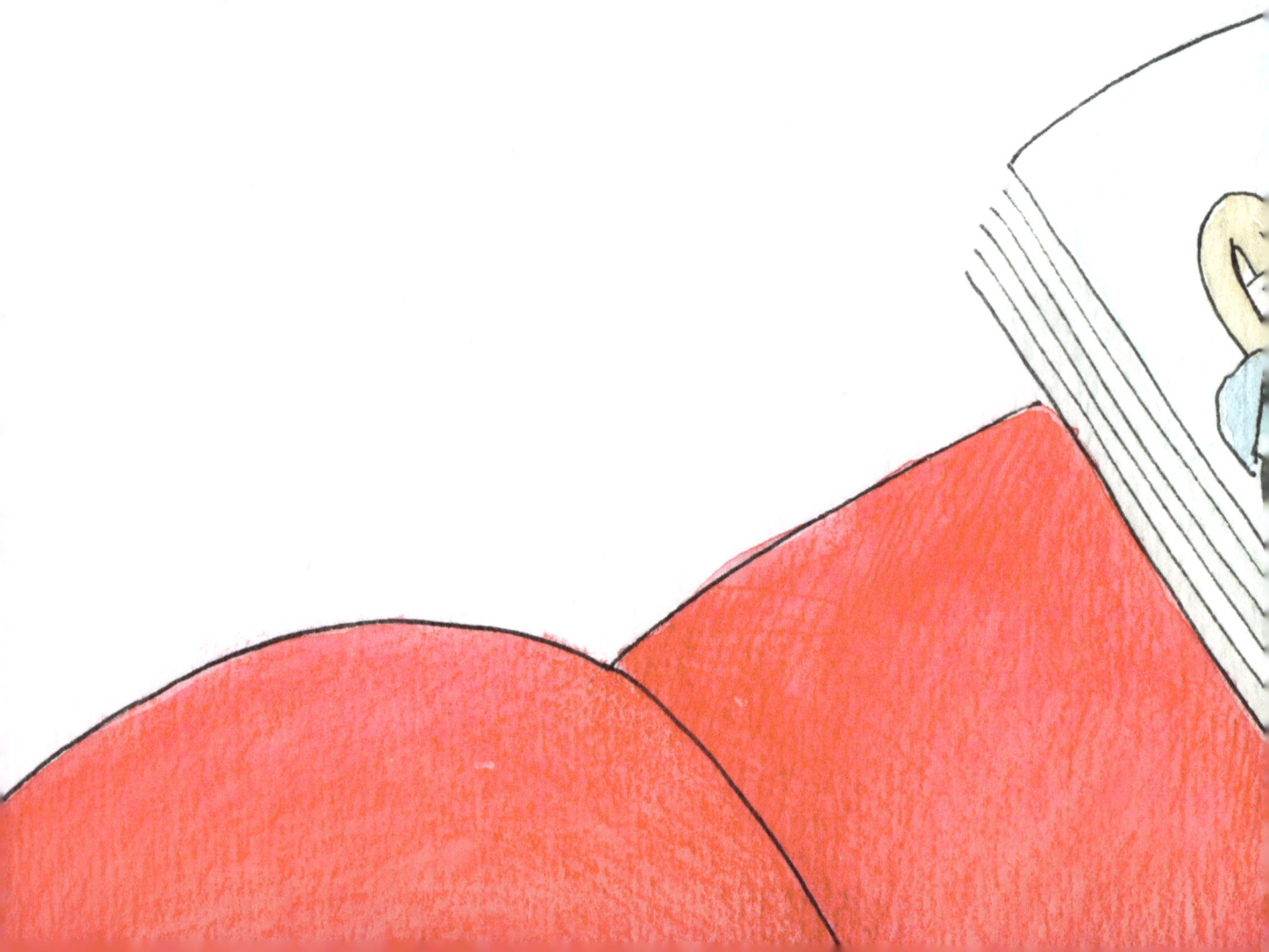

Mrs. Muggles is a cat.

She's a big, black, squinty-eyed cat.

She loves to wear glasses.

"Cats can't read," you might say.

Well, that is true. Normal cats can't read.

Mrs. Muggles is not like other cats.

She learned to read with her best friend Willow.

Willow is nine years old.

"What do cats like to do with glasses?"

Answer and glass quiz on last page of book.

When Willow was four, she began to learn
a, b, c's with her Kookum. 'Kookum' means
Grandma in Cree.

Mrs. Muggles watched Willow learn
her letters every day.

When Willow was five, she put letters together. She formed simple words like 'he, she, cat, and hat'. Mrs. Muggles loved when they learned the word 'cat.'

It was the 'purr-fect' word!

cat

When Willow was six, she learned more words in school. With the help of her teacher, Willow soon learned how to read big sentences.

Willow and her Kookum read the sentences every day after school.

Willow liked to read words out loud to her Kookum. Mrs. Muggles would listen to the words. She liked to peer over Willow's shoulder.

Or she would sit beside the book.

Mrs. Muggles would watch Willow's finger while she traced the words. Willow traced with her finger to help Mrs. Muggles learn how to read.

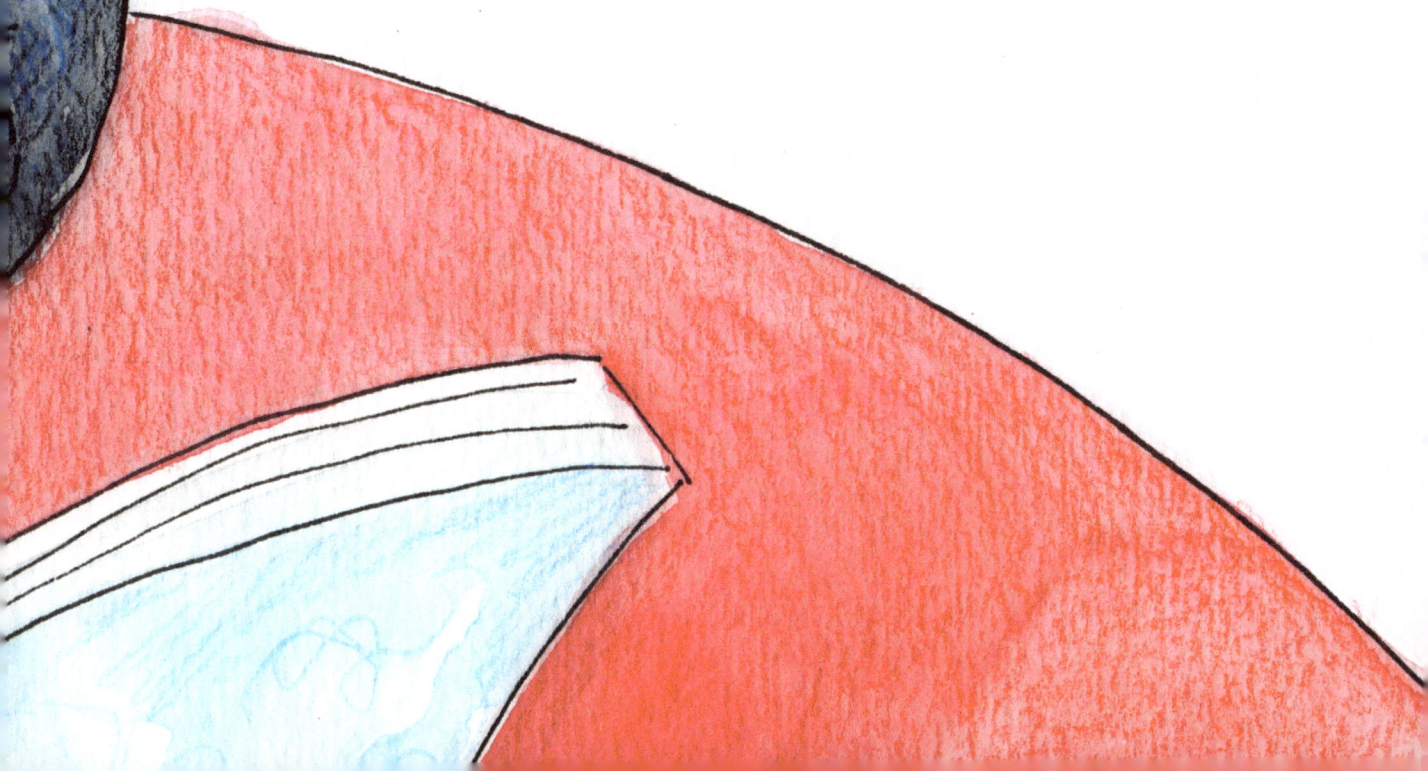

When Willow was seven, Mrs. Muggles could read

words and letters just like Willow.

Mrs. Muggles loves Mondays and Fridays.

On Mondays, Willow signs out one book from her school library.

On Fridays, Willow goes to the library with her Dad. She signs out three books at the local library.

Willow is thrilled when her Kookum
or Mom gives her a book for a present.

Willow loves books.

When Willow is done reading, she leaves her
book open. Books are left on the table, the big
red chair, the sofa, or her bed.

Mrs. Muggles thinks this is 'purr-fect.'

She races to get a pair of her reading glasses. Then Willow puts them on for her. Willow loves to buy Mrs. Muggles fancy glasses.

When Mrs. Muggles reads, she turns to the first page of the book. She looks at the pictures then begins to read the story.

She likes the story where a little girl makes new friends when she starts school. She loves the book where a Cree boy shows his little brother how to fish.

Then there is the story about a bird that longs to be free of its cage. Willow reads a lot of books about toys that talk to each other.

Mrs. Muggles likes those stories too.

Willow reads all kinds of books.

Some are happy. There are silly stories with funny people in them. Other books take people on adventures. Then there are lots of books with nature and animals in them.

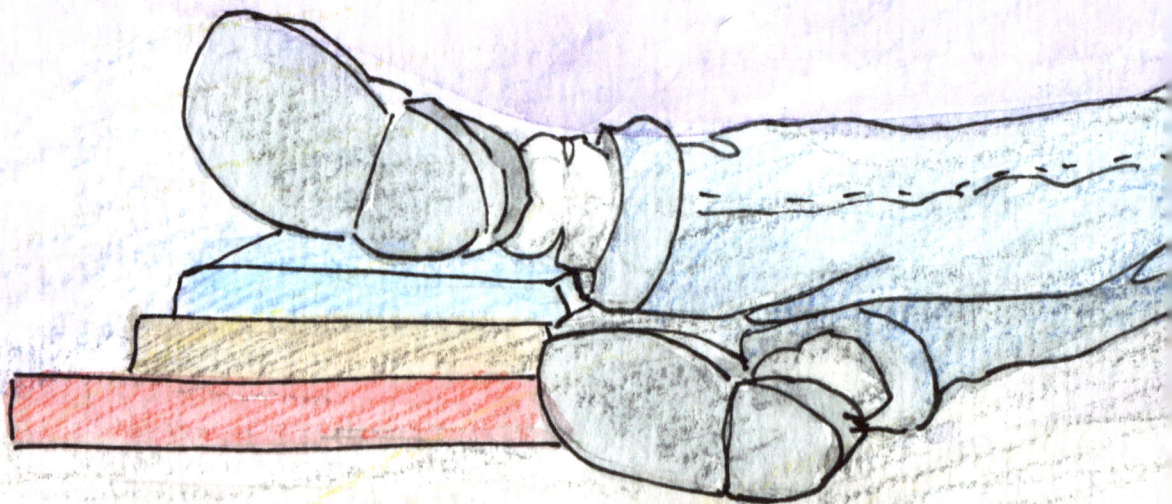

Willow loves to read legends. In these books, animals and birds teach children about nature and the earth. People also learn how to be kind to one another.

Mrs. Muggles loves legends with animals and birds in them. She can read legends all day long.

Now that she is older, Willow leaves a book open for her best friend every day. Willow puts a new book on the sunny red chair in the corner of the living room before she goes to school. This is Mrs. Muggles' reading spot.

The next challenge for Mrs. Muggles is to read Willow's chapter books. She hopes Willow picks chapter books with lots of pictures in them.

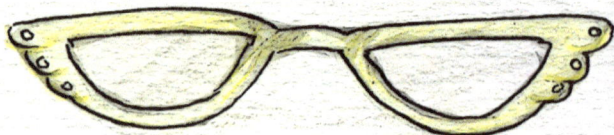

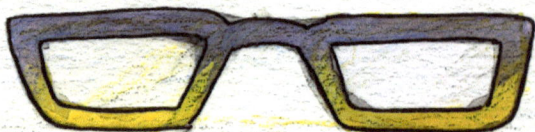

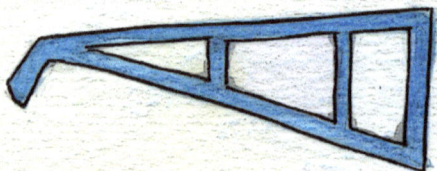

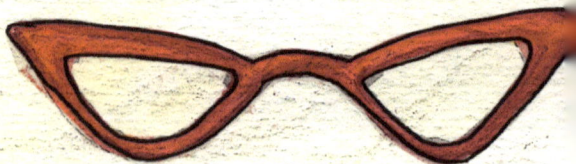

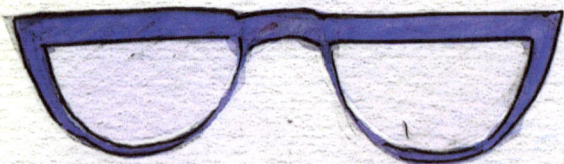

"What do cats like to do with glasses?"

Cats like to play with glasses and bite them like a chew toy. Mrs. Muggles likes to wear her glasses though.

Quiz

Mrs. Muggles and her friends are wearing glasses on most pages of the story. Go back and match a pair of glasses from this page with the ones worn by Mrs. Muggles and her friends.

Glossary:

Kookum (sounds like Kooh-gum) – Grandma

Cree – One of the largest groups of First Nations/Native Americans in North America. There are about 200,000 members who live in Canada and the Northern United States.

www.ingramcontent.com/pod-product-compliance
Lightning Source LLC
Chambersburg PA
CBHW042125040426
42450CB00002B/73